What peop
about Don ~~~~ ~p...

I've known Josh for many years, and his book has truly inspired and challenged me to dream bigger. He gives readers a transparent look into his road to success and takes us on a journey to discover purpose life and love!

—**Gabe Salazar (Actor and National Speaker)**

Upon meeting Josh, you realize that joy resides and good hearted and genuine people do exist. Upon reading his story you understand God's faithfulness to carry us to the point of fulfillment regardless of the path we must travel in our journey. God has not given up on you, don't give up on Him. Within these pages is HOPE, a hope that will not disappoint. So read, receive and breathe again.

—**Camy "Cameron" Arnett (Actor, Author, Speaker, Filmmaker)**
CEO, Camy Arnett Production Studios Founder, Saving Destinies

Don't Give Up is an incredible story that will inspire, motivate, and challenge you to keep moving forward. Josh does an incredible job illustrating the hardships that he has faced throughout life. Even in the most bleak of circumstances, Josh places his faith in God above all else and is now able to use his testimony to inspire others. Even when all odds are stacked against you, trust God and don't give up!

—**Randall Sean Garcia**
(Pastor, Founder of The Christian Leadership Network)

Josh's story is beyond inspiring. It tells us what the heart is capable of regardless of what life throws at us. Starting with the hardships and heartbreaks of his childhood, his circumstances could have easily put him on a path of anger and self-pity. Instead the early seeds of prayer by his mother and the love of his family put him on a course that would not only see him achieve many milestones but encourage and motivate so many along the way. His love for life, family and God are contagious. I have had the pleasure of witnessing Josh achieve the impossible many times. His story will inspire you to dust off your dreams, begin again, one step at a time always looking for God's light on your path.

—Phil Sillas (Award-winning Producer, Songwriter)

I've known Josh for many years and his testimony has always inspired me. He is a refined product of his journey and now he is a vessel of the Lord being used to bless many. I'm so glad that this life story is now in print and I know it will inspire all that read it. I highly recommend this book to anyone, especially someone who is disheartened or discouraged.

—Ray Jones
(Radiance Ministries, Author, Worship Pastor, National Speaker)

DON'T GIVE UP

DON'T GIVE UP

From homelessness to a purpose-filled life, the inspiring story of believing in a dream and never giving up

JOSH LOPEZ

Published in association with JL Music.

Scripture quotations from *The Message by Eugene H. Peterson* 1993, 1994, 1995, 1996, 2000.

Library of Congress Cataloging-in-Publication Data

Lopez, Josh D.
Don't Give Up/Josh Lopez
1. Motivational 2. Inspirational

Art Design by Chris Sanchez
Photography by Justin Ellis
Graphic art: Chris Sanchez
Book editor: Staci Frenes (Grammar Boss)
Book editor: Stephanie Harrison
Interior design: Ines Monnet (Ines | Book Formatter)
Photographs on pages 33, 46, 77, 109, 115, 127: Eva Magana Photography
© 2020 Josh Lopez

ISBN 978-1-71612-519-5 (hardcover)
ISBN 979-8-65665-368-8 (paperback)
ISBN 978-0-578-67750-7 (ebook)

For Worldwide Distribution. Printed in the U.S.A.

Dedicated to Martha, Joshua, Cristian and Sofia.

You are my why.

You inspire me to work hard and

to never give up on our dreams!

In loving memory of my Dad, Josue Lopez

Table of Contents

INTRODUCTION

Whenever you set out to accomplish any dream in life for the first time you take giant leaps of faith. You also step outside of your comfort zone and learn so much in the process. Publishing this book is a dream come true for me, and I am honored that you would share this journey with me. I have learned so much in the process of writing my story, and I'm grateful you decided to read it. It is my hope, more than anything, that you would be inspired and encouraged by the stories and life lessons in this book.

This book is for the kid in all of us who still believes in superheroes, fairy tales, and miracles. It is for the person who chooses to never lose sight of hope, and for the one who somehow lost hope along the journey. It's for the mom, dad, son, daughter, or friend who wants to live their life intentionally, with no regrets, and to leave a significant legacy for their family. It's for the wise, elderly man or woman who has accepted that perhaps it is too late to fulfill their dreams, and for the person who is weary and thinking of stopping their race. It's for everyone who has ever felt the pain of brokenness and the weight of crushing defeat, and for those who have been knocked down and wondered whether they should get back up.

I will share stories that start with impossibilities and end in this truth: everything is possible if you believe. I will share some of my favorite miracles of how God took a broken, hopeless, angry, messed-up young man and gave him hope, success, purpose, and, most of all, unconditional love.

As you read these pages, I hope that your heart embraces courage, and that the fire inside of you reignites and fills you with zeal for your future. I want to encourage you to live your life beyond every limit that you or anyone else has set in front of you. You are here for a greater purpose than you realize, and much bigger than what is in front of you right now. Your life is not an accident, and I believe with all my heart that every mistake plays a big part in your destiny. You were made on purpose by a divine creator who had great dreams in mind when He made you.

I'd like to take you on a journey with me through the most difficult times in my life and share with you how I was able to overcome challenging obstacles. I have put my heart and soul in every chapter and I hope you are inspired reading every word. I believe that God puts seeds in our path to help us get to our destiny. I pray that you will embrace these words as seeds for your destiny, and that they grow and flourish into giant-sized dreams realized. I pray you can take everything you have learned and inspire someone else to never give up on their dreams.

I hope that when you read this book you feel surrounded by thousands of friends cheering you on and shouting three simple but life-altering words: "DON'T GIVE UP!" As you read this book, be open to possibility. More than anything, I desire for you to have a new meaningful purpose in your life, and to be inspired to share that with many others. Thank you for joining me on this journey.

For you created my inmost being;

you knit me together in my mother's womb.

I praise you because I am fearfully and wonderfully made;

your works are wonderful,

I know that full well.

My frame was not hidden from you

when I was made in the secret place,

when I was woven together in the depths of the earth.

Your eyes saw my unformed body;

all the days ordained for me were written in your book

before one of them came to be.

How precious to me are your thoughts, oh God!

How vast is the sum of them!

Were I to count them,

they would outnumber the grains of sand—

When I awake, I am still with you.

Psalm 139:13-18 (Message Bible)

CHAPTER 1

Each of us is carefully made, uniquely created and designed with an intentional purpose.

AN OCEAN OF DREAMS

In early February of 2019 I was invited to sing on a cruise ship and share my life story. My team and I were on our way to Mahogany Bay, Belize and Key west, Florida. Being able to travel all over the world and sing in front of thousands of people was a dream come true for me. I had experienced so many beautiful moments in which I was able to use what God gave me to give hope to others through music—it was my passion, calling and life mission. Getting to do what I love with the people I love filled my heart with great joy.

On this particular trip, we sang every night at the top of our lungs, amazed to see God move on people's hearts. I shared my story a few times, and for some it brought tears of joy. Sharing the stage that week were some of my favorite musical artists, actors and amazing filmmakers. Many moments I found myself looking up and saying, *Thank you, God! Thank you, Lord, for saving me, for redeeming me, for restoring me, for giving me purpose.* So many of my dreams realized, and a life that was beyond my dreams. I had to pinch myself, because I felt like I was dreaming. That, to me, was truly living out my dreams: being awake in my dreams.

I decided that trip was the perfect time to finish the final chapters of this book that took me years to write. I was surrounded by the Atlantic Ocean for five days, doing what I loved. I couldn't help but look at my life and feel incredibly grateful for all of the dreams that God had granted me. God, through His rich grace, had brought me to this amazing moment where I did not doubt for a second that I was doing what I was placed on this earth to do.

Why was this so profound to me? It was all a matter of perspective. I had experienced the complete opposite thoughts and feelings years before—thoughts that perhaps all of us have had at one time or another: *What am I on this earth for? What is my purpose? Will I ever do what I love to do for a living? How are these problems going to work out? When will the pain of being let down stop? Will I ever see the dream in my heart come to pass?* Those thoughts, many years before, were what made the present moment so special. God had completely shifted all of my past fears and replaced them with confidence and passion. I was doing what I'd always longed to do, what I had hoped to do all of my life, and it felt amazing!

One afternoon we finished our concert early and I decided to sit on the balcony in my room and spend some time with God, reflecting on all that had happened that day. I looked out at the deep blue ocean; it was breathtaking. Countless reflections of the sun glinted across the giant waves as they crashed, one by one, over each other. The sound brought peace and calm. I thought of the times as a kid when dreams seemed as endless as the picture right in front of me. An ocean of wishes and hopes, with endless possibilities. I realized I had never stopped dreaming, and although at times I wanted to give up, God never gave up on me. He had always been faithful to remind me that He placed every 'God dream' in my heart, and would help me accomplish those big ones that seemed so out of reach.

Looking out at the ocean, I also had time to reflect on the rough seas and turbulent waters I'd had to overcome. I remembered times when I left the comfort of the shore and ventured into the unknown, sometimes feeling as if I was sinking and almost drowning. God rescued me every time and reminded me that he would carefully piece this together as a part of my journey. He would use every single mistake, every wound, and even the most painful failures to make me stronger. I didn't see it then but in that present moment it was as clear as the air I was breathing.

I saw countless parallels between my life and the ocean: leaving the shore, crashing waves, troubled waters, peaceful sunsets, beautiful calm waters, deep unknown seas, endless grace—all of it made life beautiful and each one taught me something that would change the way I view my purpose in life.

That evening, the beautiful truth of one of my favorite verses in the Bible resonated with me. Psalm 139: *Like an open book, you watched me grow from conception to birth; all the stages of my life were spread out before you, the days of my life all prepared before I'd even lived one day. Your thoughts-how rare, how beautiful! I couldn't even begin to count them, any more than I could count the sands of the sea.*

I love this profound truth! God has always had a plan for my life and yours, designed with the same attention to detail that it took to create every single fiber of our being. The human body has 207 bones and 37.2 trillion cells, to name a few of the details that our creator saw to in creating us, so it would make sense that this same creator placed specific dreams in our hearts to accomplish His plan and purpose on this earth.

Each of us is carefully made, uniquely created and designed with an intentional purpose.

Looking out at the beautiful ocean that day took me once again to a place of overwhelming gratitude. I took a deep breath as I reflected on God's incredible goodness in my life. I knew it had taken many painful and beautiful factors to get me there, but the greatest was, and always will be, God's amazing love. Through the sound of crashing waves and a breathtaking sunset I heard the familiar words that continue to resonate in my heart to this day: *Don't give up.* I was reminded again that God's grace for us, and His never relenting commitment to us becoming all that He created us to be, is as constant as the waves in the ocean.

This is my journey. This is my story.

CHAPTER 2

The happiest moments I remember as a kid always involved music and family.

TROUBLED WATERS

My dad, Josue Lopez Claudio, and my mom, Yolanda Alvarez, met in the late 1960s, when they were young, adventurous and full of big dreams. Our country was at war in Vietnam and my brave dad had just returned from fighting for our country; he was just a 19-year-old kid when he had left for war. Both strong and wounded, he'd grown up with an abusive father, part of the reason he wanted to get out and explore the world as a young man. My mom, one of the youngest of eight siblings, lived in a small town and grew up on a ranch. A gifted singer with a love for music and adventure, she had just received an opportunity to study classical music at 16 years old

19

when she met my dad. The two
had great chemistry and quickly
fell for each other.

The war had brought a
sense of urgency and disparity
for young people. The culture
said: if you feel like doing something, don't waste time, just do
it. It was with this mindset, and
the love they had for each other,
that they decided to elope and
get married. It was a classic love story. They were young
and full of dreams for a bright future together. Although it
was a turbulent time with the war in Vietnam, one event in
particular gave people hope: Neil Armstrong became the
first astronaut to set foot on the moon and fulfill President
John F. Kennedy's pledge to land a man on the moon by
the end of the decade. Young people like my mom and dad
were inspired to belief that miracles could happen, and to
hope that there could be a better tomorrow for them and
their generation.

After getting married they decided to move to my dad's
birthplace, Puerto Rico, where his dad owned a small gro-

cery store, and where my dad hoped to one day take over the family business. My mom had never traveled outside of Texas, so this was the greatest adventure she had ever experienced. They moved to Puerto Rico with no real plan in place, and at first it was adventurous and fun, like most things when you are just living for the moment. Puerto Rico is one of the most beautiful islands in the world, a place where everything feels dreamy. The island is surrounded by breathtaking oceans and filled with a sense of adventure. But it wasn't long before reality set in for my young parents.

A few months after moving to Puerto Rico, they learned that my grandfather's family business was not doing as well as my dad thought. It was a very tough time in Puerto Rico, economically, and my grandfather wasn't able to pay for the store, which meant my dad's plan to stay on in the business wasn't going to work. It was not what they had hoped for and they began to struggle, barely making ends meet. They didn't know what they were going to do. My dad found odd jobs and worked hard to provide for them but it was a very rocky start.

In addition to financial hardship, there was another mountain they faced in their first years of marriage, which proved to be the toughest they would ever have to climb. My dad, like many soldiers who returned from Vietnam, suffered from PTSD, post-traumatic stress disorder. When they experienced setbacks, he would go into panic attacks and fear would grip his heart, affecting both of them greatly. With each disappointment, it was as if the world was burning and crashing down, sending my dad into a deep depression. In the late 1960s and early 1970s, there was no real diagnosis or treatment for soldiers suffering from this mental and emotional pain. As a result, many soldiers and families were being torn apart.

My parents needed a miracle, and received one when they found out they were going to have their first child within a year of being married. This was such good news, and yet they were also not sure how they would be able to make it. When my oldest sister, Ruth, was born, it brought so much joy to my parents and became a blessing and their saving grace. Although life still had its challenges, baby Ruth was their little sweet angel sent from heaven and they were absolutely in love with her. Her life gave them a renewed vision to make things work. Happy as they were, my dad worked hard to provide but could not seem to hold on to a job.

The next few years were very tough financially, with my dad still going in and out of his battle with PTSD. It seemed to progress for the worse, since my dad still had received no diagnosis or clinical treatment. I was born in 1973 in Bayamon, Puerto Rico, and my mom was thrilled that now they had both a little boy and girl. Despite the financial and emotional difficulties they faced, their children gave them so much hope.

Soon after I was born, my dad had an opportunity to go back to school in New York, so they decided to move to the Bronx, New York. This was a huge sacrifice for them, but they looked at it with the hope that it would pay off in the future. We moved to a tiny apartment in a poor, rough neighborhood in South Bronx, New York and in the next few years we grew to a family of eight with six kids. We didn't own a TV or any electronics, but life was full of creativity. We were those barefooted kids, playing in the street until late at night, making up games, jumping into fire hydrants. We loved being outside. Even though it was a rough neighborhood, everyone looked out for each other and we learned to be tough kids.

Music was a big part of my childhood, and I developed a passion for it at a young age. Dad was a skilled musician and Mom a classical singer. She sang like an angel and taught my sisters and I to sing. She would take us to a small church where we learned to sing Spanish hymns known as 'coritos.' I loved seeing people's reaction when they were inspired

or touched by music. I felt the music deep in my soul, and often it was an escape from my rough childhood. We would sing at church and always had music in our home. Dad would invite his friends over to play salsa music, with everyone playing percussive instruments such as congas, bongos, or even pots and pans, until the early hours of the morning. We would watch and sometimes join these parties my dad called rumbas, though my mom was not a fan of this on school nights.

We would take it all in, this beautiful music. My brother, Tommy, definitely inherited Dad's gift of rhythm, whereas I followed Mom's love for singing. I didn't realize it at the time, but my parents were teaching us a great deal about music and life. I was learning that no matter how tough life could be, you could still find joy through music and family.

The happiest moments I remember as a kid always involved music and family. The lack of material things helped us develop our creativity.

Going without electricity and water at times was difficult but we found ways to make the best of it, and we developed strength because of it.

In addition to being musical, growing up in a big family in the South Bronx made me a tough kid. When I fell, it took a lot for me to cry. My mom always taught us to get back up. She was, and is to this day, my rock. We experienced some traumatic things growing up: seeing people on drugs, who at the time I thought were just crazy people; having to defend my sisters and get into fights; walking miles to school and every other place we needed to go since we didn't have a car. In the midst of the craziness around us, we were always watching out for each other. My siblings all had different personalities, but I was always trying to lead and be the boss. Always trying to act older than my age, I was a mini-dad at times to my sisters. When we fought it was heated, but when we reconciled, it was quick.

We were stronger at a young age than most kids, but those experiences sometimes left deep wounds. Among those was a memory that I will never forget. I was six years old, on a playground, and I watched a young woman who was high on heroin leap from a 15-story building. It was the first time I had ever seen someone take their own life. After it happened, I remember having lots of bad dreams, and the concept of death became very real to me. Even though my mom worked so hard to protect us, there were things I experienced that left deep wounds and scars.

I learned a lot about life and overcoming hardships when I was growing up. I learned to appreciate the smallest of things. When we had nice meals, we were beyond grateful. When our water and electricity were working, we were thankful. There were Christmas holidays where my parents didn't have money to buy us gifts, but we appreciated what we had.

Over time, my dad's condition progressively got worse, and it was hard on all of us. He never found the right help for his PTSD—like many soldiers during that time—as the Veteran's Administration was (and still is) a broken system. Dad would get angry over our financial situation and become more and more abusive with Mom. As a kid, I always saw my dad stressed, sad and angry. The only time I remember him being happy was when he was playing music or when we were not under financial stress. But my mom had a special gift of patience and meekness. She was the most humble and gentle person I have ever known, and she stood by his side during the many rough times, continuing to believe that he could change. This is where I first saw unconditional love displayed; my mother was teaching me about the strength of humility through her example.

A small change did come when I was a teenager—my dad decided to move our family from the Bronx to Texas. He had a job opportunity to be a forklift driver for a start-up tech company in Austin, and he was eager to get our family out of that bad neighborhood. But sadly, after receiving the offer and moving us to Austin to start over, he got angry with his employer and quit. That start-up company went on to become Dell Computer! I often think God was trying to bless my dad so many times, but it was hard for him to just stay the course. He lived with a lot of pain and regret. Wounded, he swept everything under the rug and continued to struggle emotionally.

Dad began battling with drug addiction to numb the pain of his past. I realize now that so much of it was caused by never dealing with what he went through in Vietnam, and never getting the right help for PTSD and other issues he had faced as a kid. Even though he was not perfect, he was a hard worker and he was tough. At the time, he was my superhero. So, when I found out that my dad was a heroin addict, it crushed me. I was so angry I couldn't even cry. I felt a sense of betrayal and hopelessness. I was afraid of him becoming one of those crazy people I remembered seeing when we lived in Bronx, New York. I started to build a wall between us; I didn't want to talk to my dad or see him.

In Austin, we began to lose everything—including a place to live. My family became homeless, staying at motels when we could afford it, and going to school in the same clothes we had worn the day before: ripped shoes and sometimes the same jeans for a week. My sister and I skipped lunch when we didn't have money to eat, and we would hang out in front of the library for the entire lunch hour. There was no time for extracurricular activities like sports or band, it was school and then finding out where we were going to spend the night. We had an old minivan at the time and stored all of our belongings in that van, even sleeping in it when we didn't have money for a motel room.

My mom, through it all, still had faith that we would come out strong. She seemed to never waiver in her trust in God. I am sure she cried and experienced a lot of pain but she was always careful to be strong for us, her six kids. She stood in lines seeking government help and worked odd jobs to provide for us. We were able to find a small house on the east side of Austin through government assistance. When I was thirteen, my dad left for a year and I would walk for miles to apply at different places for work. My first job was at a pizza place where a kind lady let me sweep the parking lot for free pizza. I didn't realize it at the time, but I was learning about how to work hard, and the fulfilling feeling of being rewarded for that hard work. Nothing was easy and that was building yet more strength in me. I was a tough kid. I had to be.

Dad returned after a year and Mom helped him get the help he needed. She still loved him and had great faith that he could be a restored man., but the problem was that my dad didn't seem to want to be restored. She was the one rescuing him, getting him help, checking him into a detox center, and praying for him. He never finished his treatment, and ended up coming back home. I was angry at my dad and had a hard time accepting that he had changed. I blamed our entire situation on him, and didn't have much respect for him after he had left us the year before.

My anger finally came out one night and we got into a huge fight. My dad kicked me out of the home we had worked so hard to get with government assistance. He also said some very hurtful words that crushed me. I ran out and walked aimlessly for miles until I ended up in downtown Austin. I was just a teenager but I had no plans to return home. I was too hurt and stubborn. What I didn't realize is that my heart was getting numb over time. I desperately wanted to just be free of the pain I had in my heart. I wanted to stop feeling angry, hurt and confused.

The most painful part was that I was starting to lose my faith in God. It was as if I had lost faith in my dad years before and now had come to a point where I had lost faith in God. I thought, *How could God allow us to go through so much pain, how could He allow my dad to kick me out and reject me?* My image of my dad slowly became the image that I had of God. I thought if I was not good, I would not be loved. This would affect many of the choices I was about to make, and I was about to discover rock bottom at a very young age.

CHAPTER 3

My mom had always taught us that there was good and evil. Both would fight for our life and it was up to us to choose.

HITTING ROCK BOTTOM

Here I was, a homeless 16-year-old kid sleeping on a bench in downtown Austin, who had dropped out of high school and didn't want anything to do with my dad. But we had been homeless before, so I had learned some useful things about how to survive. For example, I learned that I could go to motels early in the morning and get free breakfast. I knew that I could use hotel restrooms. I learned that the Salvation Army offered cots if it was cold and raining outside. I also learned that I had to take it day by day. Returning home was not an option for me. I learned to mask the reality of what was going on in my heart: I was too broken, angry and extremely stubborn. It was the early 90s and most people didn't have cell phones or social media, Facebook or Instagram. People didn't keep up with each other's stories, so you could go dark really quickly. My day-to-day life went by unseen by friends or family and I sunk into a very dark place, very fast.

I spent the next couple of years without any contact with my family. I hustled and did whatever I needed to do to get by. There were days I felt like my life was over, and even had suicidal thoughts. There were other days where I thought something miraculous would happen that would change everything. I slept on street corners and at the Salvation Army. Every morning at 2 a.m. it was the same thing: people would turn into belligerent and obnoxious human beings. I once saw another homeless person die of an overdose. The days were filled with hopelessness, sadness, depression, loneliness, and fear. It was as if I had fallen into a giant deep hole and I didn't know how I would ever climb out.

I was convinced that no one cared or even knew where I was, and that my life was almost over. The world was cruel. This was evident when I saw people drink to numb their pain. One night, two men were arguing, and clearly both were drunk. One of my friends tried to step in and hold them back and was stabbed by one of the men. I don't remember ever crying, my heart just got harder. Everyone was lost and searching. Everyone was carrying some type of pain. I spent Christmas as a homeless teenager and got to see the world from a different perspective. I would sit for hours on a bench as people walked by, feeling invisible, hopeless, sad and lost. Just a teenager, and I was already hitting rock bottom.

Yet, hope was not completely lost. There was something in me that I believe my mom instilled, buried deep down under all the pain: hope and a belief that my life would somehow change.

I knew I had to do something. I knew I couldn't live the rest of my life this way. I later learned that this was God's grace protecting me and throwing out a life vest every time I was about to drown.

My mom had always taught us that there was good and evil. Both would fight for our life and it was up to us to choose.

That truth kept me from doing cocaine and heroin on several occasions when I was tempted. I also was afraid of what it could do to me, as I saw drug addiction as my dad's demon.

One thing my dad taught me was to work hard and hustle. He had been a janitor, a forklift driver, and a carpenter, and I learned from him to work hard and never ask for a handout. My mentality at that age drove me to want to be successful at something and show the world that I could bounce back from this. But every morning reality would slowly settle in. It had been close to a year that I'd been homeless, and it was now winter in Austin. I decided to ask for a job at a clothing store in the mall. The manager, who I believe now was an angel sent by God, saw something in me and gave me a job. I didn't tell her I was homeless. I managed to appear like just another badly dressed, scruffy kid with a big desire to work. After a few months at that job, I was able to get an apartment with some of my coworkers.

Having a place to live and a job afforded me a lot of freedom. My vice became dating older women—they were attracted to the tough young man from the streets. The relationships were shallow and physical. I would intentionally go into relationships just to see what I could get out of them. It was selfish but it also allowed me to keep my guard up—I was not ready to let anyone in. The women I dated were looking for someone they could fix or save. I was not ready nor did I want to be saved. I was getting further away from finding purpose and love. I was off the streets and now, living with some roommates, but I was still lost. I had basically just moved from one unhealthy situation to another.

No matter where I went, I could not escape the issues I had deep in my heart. I was still hurting, still angry, still fearing rejection and still did not have self-worth. That is the way darkness and pain work: they don't change just because you get a job, a few friends and a place to live. Even then, I knew that if I continued on this path it would only lead to a tragic outcome. What I didn't realize at the time is that if I continued, I was going to repeat history. My dad had made many of these same choices when he was younger and I was following in his footsteps. Looking back, pain has always proven to be a motivator in my life. Sometimes it motivated me to do the wrong thing and sometimes, the right thing. Little did I know, the pain I was about to feel would finally drive me to do something right.

I was dating a woman who was a dancer at a club when I was about 18. I came home from work early one day and caught my best friend sleeping with her. At first I wanted to fight him, but then something came over me and I just walked out, almost in relief. It was as if I needed something like that to happen so I could see the world I was living in for what it was. This was probably the best thing that could have happened to me at the time, and a direct result of the poor choices that I was making, especially the circle that I was surrounding myself with. Bad circle + bad choices = bad life. Good circle + good choices = good life. I was definitely in that bad circle: I had a job but was spending the

CHAPTER 4

When you're in so much pain, you have to get to the point where you just don't want to feel the same way anymore.

THE TURNING TIDES

I was tired of how I had been living over the past years and I desperately wanted to change. I had to do something different to get a different result. It sounds pretty simple but it proved to be the hardest thing.

When you're in so much pain, you have to get to the point where you just don't want to feel the same way anymore.

I had learned to patch up my wounds very carefully, but I was still bleeding and needed to change. It was time.

I decided that the antidote to my deep-rooted hurt and pain was to become successful. From my perspective, everything that remotely resembled pain was a direct result of poverty. What I didn't understand was that my soul was broken and I was only trying to fix what was on the outside. I had no idea what I was going to do to become successful, but somehow in my mind 'success' was equated with not struggling financially the way I had been for years.

Success, to my young mind, meant several things. It meant that I could afford to buy what I wanted, and travel wherever I wanted. It meant being able to enjoy my freedom, and live the adventures and dreams that I had as a kid—like being able to make a living out of music, and to have some type of business. And like most guys, I wanted to meet a dream girl I could spend the rest of my life with and have a family.

It was a huge turning point for me to have the opportunity to go back to school and move in with my gracious aunt and uncle in Puerto Rico. I felt I was getting another shot at

a lot of things.

I finished my GED, and although I had two jobs I really wanted to go to college. It was hard to get in but I was determined and able to get a government grant. I knew what it felt like to want something so bad and go after it, and started to work my way through college. Over the next two years I worked hard, as my constant motivation was to never return to where I had been. Success was non-negotiable. I finished college with a 4.0 GPA and graduated valedictorian of my class. That was a beautiful moment; I felt so accomplished. Just a few years after being homeless, I was a college graduate and first in my class.

That victory inspired more confidence. I was asked to participate in a contest called *Mr. Puerto Rico,* which was funny to me at the time but I was looking at it from the standpoint of making more money and being successful—this was a way I could get there. I met a lot of interesting people, and though it was a very fake world I had been around that kind of thing before. But it was also different, because the producers and sponsors were very wealthy and seemed to want to put a lot of emphasis on the outer appearance. There was a talent show for the contestants and I decided to write and sing my own song. No one knew I could sing so this came as a shocker to the judges and producers. I struggled with confidence in this area because I had never really done anything professionally with my musical talents before, but that night after I sang, I got a standing ovation.

Again, more doors were opening for me. As I walked off stage that night, a music producer approached me and asked if I was interested in auditioning for a pop group. I had no idea who he was, but it turns out he was a manager for one of the most popular bands in Latin America, and represented groups like Menudo and Garibaldi. I went and sang for the audition and was offered my first record contract. Over the next year, I was the lead singer for a touring Latin pop group, opening for famous acts. We had a hit single playing on the radio and everywhere I went in Puerto Rico, people knew who we were. This was very different from the homeless boy sitting on a bench, feeling invisible.

I felt like I was on top of the world—almost in a dream. I was doing what I loved and was so grateful because I knew that this was not my doing alone. All of the stuff I had been through as a teenager had grounded me, and this new fame I was experiencing felt a little fake.

I knew I wasn't better than anyone else. I knew that I had not arrived. I knew that people were just treating me a certain way because of how the record label painted me.

While this was all in the back of my mind, I went with it and had a good time singing. But deep down inside life still felt shallow to me.

I found myself on the other side of homelessness with a nice place near the beach, doing what I had always dreamed of doing. It was a glimpse of success, and you would think that I felt fulfilled. I felt blessed, but there were still so many issues I had not dealt with inside. Surprisingly, I knew I was missing something.

Sometimes you have to experience having nothing and then having something to realize the *real* something that you need.

This would only make sense to me later. Life was different now: I could buy what I wanted, travel, and was on my way to being a successful artist. But I couldn't help but pause from time to time and try to understand why I still felt empty inside. I knew love was the most important thing, and I still had not found this. Everyone I had surrounded myself with just told me what I wanted to hear; they were just there for the success.

Everything I was doing pointed to me, yet I lacked purpose and deep inside I knew this. My mom had taught me
when I was very young that all of us have been put on this
earth to fulfill a specific purpose. We each carry a unique
fingerprint that marks us and sets us apart. But I was still
living in brokenness and selfishness, and I knew at some
point I would have to deal with my anger and hurt from my
childhood and teenage experiences. Sometimes the harsh
reality of seeing ourselves as we are propels us to the most
incredible moments when we decide that we don't want
to be that way anymore. So, even though I thought my tide

had turned toward success—the real turning tide in my life was still about to happen.

It happened when my sister Ruth came to visit me in Puerto Rico. We sat at a restaurant, talking, and I thought she was going to be so impressed with how well I had done for myself. I had every intention of impressing her, and somehow believed she would tell Dad that I had accomplished great things so he would be proud of me. Wrong. She saw right through my façade, and right into the hurt deep in my heart. She asked if I was miserable, which was perplexing but was also refreshing, because no one had ever cared enough to ask that question. Then, what she said next changed my life forever.

Ruth shared a simple story of truth about Jesus. She told me that He sacrificed His life for me so that I could live, love and become everything that I was created for. She said it wasn't about what I could do for Jesus, but what He had already done for me. It wasn't about being perfect and following a list of rules, but it was about a relationship with Jesus. It was about truly starting to love myself, others and God. Then she showed me a verse in the Bible, John 3:16: *For God so loved the world that He gave His only begotten son, that whoever believes in Him would not perish but have everlasting life.*

She was so bold in her conviction and in the words she spoke. I had not had anyone speak the truth to me in many years. Suddenly, the fast track I was running on came to a screeching halt. Everyone else in my life had just been telling me what I wanted to hear: my music label and management team just filled my ego, my friends constantly flattered me. But my sister was calling me out. She knew I was living a facade. I sat there, finally listening to those beautiful words of truth, even though some of it was hard to take in, and I wanted to hear more. I had a purpose? I was not an accident? There is a God who knows every single detail of my life and He loves me? This was such good news to me, I needed some time to reflect on these words.

Later that night, I sat alone by the beach in Puerto Rico and said this simple prayer: *God I want this life that my sister is talking about. Please forgive me for all my bad decisions in life. Please heal me, change me. I believe.* It's hard to put into words what happened next. I hadn't cried in years but like a waterfall, the tears began to fall. It felt like a deep layer of me had been peeled away and I could finally be honest with myself and those around me. It was pure freedom. God became real to me at that moment; He had touched my heart and everything my sister told me was true. The peace I felt, the strength I felt, the love I felt, was inexplicable. It was something I had never felt before.

I was ready for real change. I realized then that success, although it was great, would not give me the happiness I was looking for. I could see that I had to deal with the pain in my heart in order to truly be free. I was ready to be born again. To live my life to the fullest. I received Jesus in my heart and that is where the journey of countless dreams was fulfilled, and the journey of finding my purpose moved to a completely new level. All the mistakes, all the brokenness, God would use to shape the next years, and the impact He allowed me to have on others.

CHAPTER 5

Happiness, peace, and love became more important to me than pursuing wealth and fame.

WAVES OF GRACE

It was a new day. The sunset was different. Everything around me began to change. My perspective, my thoughts, my ambitions and, most importantly, my heart began to change. Now I knew I had to make some practical changes in my life. I had to form new habits now that my motivation was different. I still had dreams, but my dreams were different now. I still wanted to sing, but I wanted to inspire people doing it. I still wanted to become successful but success meant being happy and finding my purpose.

Happiness, peace, and love became more important to me than pursuing wealth and fame.

I knew I wanted to do something significant with my life, I knew I wanted to help others the way others had helped me. I knew I wanted to leave a mark on this earth. And most of all, I was desperate to know the answer to the underlying question, *What is my purpose*?

I decided to move back to Austin, Texas where most of my family lived. I began working for a bank, got a one-bedroom apartment and started attending a church in Austin called Shoreline. I went to the first Wednesday of the month services and sang at the top of my lungs, so grateful for what Jesus had done in my life. I felt so much peace, happiness, and clarity. The worship pastor, a gracious and funny guy named Jerry Caldwell, heard me playing the piano in the choir room one day and came in, so I had the opportunity to share my story with him. He asked me to sing on the worship team and later asked if I would like to volunteer my time to be the worship leader for the youth at the church. I was honored that he would ask and felt like God wanted me to do this, and I was also clueless as to what to do.

This was the beginning of my journey as a worship leader. I didn't know anything about leading a band, I wasn't a good musician, all I knew was how to sing to Jesus for all that He had done for me. Thankfully, God brought many good people into my life to help me along the way. Two are dear friends that to this day I have the privilege of making music with, Jason Meekins and Aaron Kiefer. Jason and Aaron are some of the best musicians I have ever played with, but beyond that, they are true brothers and friends. I spent my days working at the bank and four nights a week volunteering at Shoreline. I was there so much that people thought I worked there. It created a sense in me that someday I actually *might* work there. I wanted to do this full-time but no real door had opened yet for that. It seemed that everything, specifically dreams, took longer than I anticipated.

One night, I attended a concert where an artist was singing and sharing his story. It sounded a lot like mine, and I was very inspired and moved by it. I said a prayer that night, asking God to use me the way He was using this person. I didn't want to be an artist or a famous singer—I had already experienced a little taste of that and it was not appealing to me anymore—I just wanted to inspire people with my story, the way that this person inspired me. I loved to encourage people, even from an early age. I felt most fulfilled when I made others feel good about themselves.

After about seven years as a volunteer worship leader, I began to wonder why I was at Shoreline. I was spinning my wheels, working very hard. I wanted to feel valued, but I felt like I wasn't being taken seriously because I was just a volunteer. I loved that place and hoped one day they would hire me so I could quit the other job I didn't like. What I didn't realize was that I was learning so much about grit, patience and not giving up.

This was one of my first "Don't Give Up" lessons: when you are meant to do something in life, it takes time for doors to open up. You have to embrace the process.

I began to think that maybe I wasn't meant to do this if I was not getting paid for it. I equated my value with how people deemed my value. This was a daily struggle for me, I started to doubt myself, I started to think that I sucked and should pursue something else in life. I had been signed to a label, I had received plenty of accolades when it came to my music, but now it was different. This had everything to do with destiny and purpose and preparing me for that.

During that time of questioning my value and purpose, I attended a concert by the same artist I had seen years before, Israel Houghton. God had already used him once to give me a glimpse of what I could do in life, so when a friend came up to me after the concert and said, "Hey, do you want to meet Israel?" I said, without any hesitation, "YES!" I wanted to tell him what an impact he had made on my life. We made our way to the front of the stage and I shook Israel's hand and began to thank him. He was very kind and sat down and we talked for a few minutes. This was super cool and it made me realize one important thing—timing. It was not a coincidence that years before, God had used him to inspire me, and now here I was being encouraged by him again at a low point in my life.

After that meeting something changed. I began to look at the possibility of traveling and singing. When talking with Israel, he was gracious enough to ask me to sing with him the following week in Florida, where he was doing a promotional tour, and I got to sing with him for the first time. This was huge! I was amazed that God had used him years before and now I was singing with him. After that first time, Israel asked if I would sing on the road with him and, of course, I said yes! I was finally seeing a breakthrough in my dream to inspire others. I didn't yet understand that the past seven years were all a part of preparing me for the next chapters in my life.

I didn't see everything in my dream happening right away, but if I took a closer look, there was something to be learned from this season, to help me get to the next.

I was becoming more skillful, stronger, focused and wiser. While I had been doubting my calling and purpose, God knew what to bring me in His timing. I was able to leave the bank that I was working for and pursue music full-time again—but this time with purpose. We toured all over the world and I learned so much traveling with amazing musicians and great leaders. We shared the stage with Kirk Franklin, Shirley Caesar, Mary Mary, The Winans and many more artists. I loved being around incredibly talented people who were doing what they loved. It's inspiring when you surround yourself with people that dream big. People with like-minded dreams help make your dreams bigger. Your capacity begins to stretch out.

Israel Houghton was becoming a household name. Aaron Lindsey, Israel's music director, was a huge inspiration and friend during this time. Watching him work behind the scenes was incredible. He was gifted, but even more, he was a true friend. One night we were doing a tour in Honduras in a packed-out stadium, and Israel turned to me after a song and said, "Share your story and a song." I hadn't expected that and was so nervous my heart started beating faster and sweat rushed down my face. I didn't know what I was going to say and had always feared public speaking, so I asked Jesus to help me. Courage filled my heart and I began to share my story for the first time in front of an audience.

I nervously went over to the piano and began playing a song I had written called, "Your Love Found Me" in Spanish. Aaron Lindsey, who was the pianist, was so gracious, saying, "Josh, you're doing good. Keep going, you got this." Aaron was more than capable to play this song without even hearing it, but instead of laughing at my very choppy playing he encouraged me. The stadium was filled with people singing the chorus. It was beautiful. I felt God's presence on my life in a way I never had before. I thought to myself, *This is what I was created to do.* After we finished the set, Israel decided to do a reprise of that song. It was so powerful and I will never forget that moment. It was one of the greatest feelings in the world, to inspire others through my story. To encourage them to live out their life to the fullest! Music was the gift that God gave me to do this and my passion grew more and more.

Over the next two years, I traveled to many places around the world. I was signed to a record label and, as if my dreams could not get any more miraculous, I was invited to the Texas governor's mansion along with seven other leaders in the community to talk about how we could give back to the community. I sat to the right of our governor and thought about being a homeless kid just years before.

It was an incredible reminder that God always had a plan for my life. That God could take me out of the darkest place and cause His light to shine on my life. It was all about sharing the hope that God had given me with as many people as possible. This became my life's purpose.

I knew I couldn't do it alone. I knew that it was God and His strength that called me to this, and that He would bring the right person to help me achieve all that He had placed me on this earth to do.

CHAPTER 6

Relationships take work, and the best relationships are the ones that have put in the work and don't always feel it.

DIVING INTO LOVE

One of my biggest desires was to find the woman that I would spend the rest of my life with. I dated quite a bit and in many of my relationships failed miserably. I was beginning to learn so many things about being the right person instead of trying to find the right person. I had always struggled with the fear of rejection, with insecurities and lots of other baggage I had never dealt with.

I hadn't yet learned that the love I desperately desired could only be found in Jesus. And that, for a dating relationship to be healthy, I needed to be complete and secure in Christ first. A relationship will only be as healthy as the health that each person brings. I was very bad at relationships and had a lot to learn. All those lessons seemed to come in the form of heartbreak. But God continued shaping me through each failure, teaching me something with every disappointment.

I decided to not date for a year and completely just dedicate my life to Jesus—I needed to take time and just work on me. For years, I had gone from one relationship to another and never really took time to deal with some deep-rooted issues. I also started going to counseling to deal with my dad's issues. I feared rejection and would sabotage a relationship because of that fear. I was learning so much about myself. I will never forget one pastor's advice when it came to finding "the one." He said,

"Everyone wants to believe that there is only one person out there for them because it is very magical. But the truth is, relationships take work, and the best relationships are the ones that have put in the work and don't always feel it."

I must admit, I was a little disappointed with this advice but it was exactly what I needed to hear at the moment. It let me know that life was not all about feelings, but about doing the right thing even when we don't feel it. This would help me later in life with relationships, work and so many other things.

It also helped me to realize that every day we are given is a gift, and we need to make the best of this time. To work hard and be consistent. Our culture today somehow makes us believe that dreams happen overnight and instantly if you are in the right place at the right time. There's no doubt that some dreams may happen this way, but in most cases, it takes a lot of work leading up to those moments.

Winning a championship happens in seconds, but there are hours and hours of sacrifice and hard work that went into getting to that moment.

I believe with all my heart that God gives us the strength and the grace to work hard for our dreams, and that we have to meet Him at the crossroads of opportunity. This means staying consistent, trusting, working hard, and being patient in the process. So, I continued doing what I knew, and just trusted that God would lead me to the one that He had for me.

I will never forget the moment when I met her. I was invited to sing at a church in San Antonio, Texas and a friend introduced me to Martha Magana, a stunningly beautiful woman he had been wanting to set me up with. I saw her from across the room and was immediately overwhelmed. She was so beautiful that I seemed to stumble over my words as I shook her hand. I could not stop looking at her. The pastor invited me to join his family for lunch, and since Martha was close to their family and was going to lunch as well, that made it an easy decision. We sat next to each other and did not even touch our food, and for me not eat the tacos in front of me was a pretty big deal! We had a lot in common and so much to talk about. I was like a high school kid on his first date with the most beautiful girl in school. I remember saying to myself as I was driving back to Austin, "God, is this my wife?"

Little did I know, she was feeling the same way. Our first date was three days later and we continued dating for the next year. Martha changed my view of how relationships could be. She helped me to believe in myself and to discover my true value. We fell in love and began studying the Bible together with a great group of friends. I had a lot of baggage but she was so patient, loving and understanding. She saw past the present into the man that God was making me. This was so different from any other relationship I had been in I was confident that this was the woman I would spend the rest of my life with.

I proposed to Martha exactly a year after we met, and we married on June 3, 2005. It was one of the best days of my life. I had spent so much of my life pursuing success and now I began to understand that the most precious and valuable thing in my life was a strong and beautiful relationship. To love and to be loved. That to me is the highest form of a dream fulfilled. To love God and know that you are loved by Him, and to love someone and not have any fear about the love they give back to you. The next years we grew together and learned much about sacrifice and giving of ourselves. It's a beautiful thing to get to enjoy dreams and share them with my soulmate. She inspired me to be better and to go after every goal with all my heart!

One day, I received an email from Phil Sillas, a legendary producer and songwriter, who is now a very close friend, from California. He said that he wanted to record a song I had written. He saw potential in it, and for me, it was the first time a successful songwriter saw potential in my songwriting. It was also the first time I heard a song I wrote being sung by someone else, an incredible artist called GB5—such a great feeling! That song went on to be recorded several times and sung by churches all over the world. To this day, I am grateful for that seed Phil Sillas planted in my musical journey. We did this several more times with songs like "God, You Are God," "O the Blood," "Not Afraid" and "Stronger Than Anything." Songwriting had become a great passion of mine, and a great way to inspire others.

Through all of this, I still had the dream of owning my own business. During one of the recording sessions in California, I asked Louie, the leader of one of the groups that was recording my song, what they did for a living because they seemed to be doing well. He said they had a window covering business that his uncle taught them when they had lost everything. I asked Louie if he would teach me the business, and if so, I would work for free. So, I extended my stay and he was kind enough to show me everything he knew about the business. I'm grateful for the Gutierrez family, for their kindness and willingness to show me this business.

When I got back to Austin, I immediately hit the ground running and started a window covering business. I had a 1995 Toyota Tacoma and would go door to door asking homeowners if they needed blinds. I hustled and did whatever I needed to do. Some days I was tempted to go back to a safe job where I knew I would get a steady income but I kept pushing. I'll never forget my first client and first paycheck; it felt wonderful and I saw great potential in this business. I learned so many things about being a business owner the hard way that first year. Things like taxes, how to resolve a manufacturer error, and how to manage time when owning your own business. In a couple of years, I had a small team and we were doing commercial jobs. I was still traveling with my music and did not want to forsake that because of business, so I began to look at it as God's way of providing for me while I did what I was passionate about, while I fulfilled my purpose.

One Day, when Martha and I were still newlyweds, Pastor Randy Philips of the gospel music group Phillips, Craig, and Dean asked me if I wanted to start a church with him. I was so honored, I said yes. I was now working a dream job at a church and starting the first years of my own business. God continued to show us His favor. Martha was working for a financial firm at the time and was very successful in what she was doing. She received an opportunity to become a partner with the firm and we moved to San Antonio.

We continued to work hard and we were certainly living out our dreams. We spent a lot of time traveling and having fun but felt the tug that there was more we could give as a couple. We had always wanted to have a family and four years into our marriage, we decided to start trying to make that dream a reality.

CHAPTER 7

God took the broken thing in our life, the thing we thought was so messed up, the thing we thought might never be fixed and made a beautiful story.

FINDING PURPOSE AT SHORE

The day my wife told me that she was pregnant was one of the most emotional and beautiful moments in my life. We began picking out names, making trips to baby stores and enjoying all of the anticipation that comes with expecting the blessing of a child. We had always dreamed of having a family and this was, as you can imagine, an incredibly happy time in our lives. Four months passed and my wife called one day to tell me she could not stop bleeding. Nothing could have prepared us for the news we were about to receive from our doctor: the baby was not going to make it.

I will never forget the brokenness we felt. My wife could not stop crying, and I tried to be strong for her but I had moments where I'd break down too. We were so hurt, broken and confused. We had so many questions and so many emotions. *Why God? Why?* In the midst of our grief, the doctor told us we might never be able to have babies in the future. There was so much sadness, but even during this storm we found hope. God surrounded us with a group of strong friends and family that helped us start the healing process. We began to trust God and His plan. We knew that whatever brokenness we were experiencing, He was well capable of putting those broken pieces back together again. Our faith was tested in such a great way.

During that difficult time, I was working on my second album with my friend, Mark Townsend. We wrote a song called, "God, You are God." The chorus lyrics are, *God, you are God even when I can't feel you, God, you are God even when I can't see you and I will worship, I will worship you.* Those lyrics were so true! No matter what we felt or had experienced in that time of difficult loss, God was still God and He was still in control of our destiny. We took a deep breath and began to hope again.

A year later, we received a call from my aunt in Florida telling us that our 3-month-old nephew, Joshua, needed a mommy and daddy. They were getting ready to put him in foster care, as Joshua's mom was on her way to rehabilitation for a drug addiction she was battling. You can only imagine all the emotions we experienced after getting off that phone call, but one thing was for sure, we knew that God was calling us to be Joshua's mommy and daddy. We knew that Joshua needed to be rescued. The next few hours were filled with many unknowns and emotions as we prepared to get on a plane and meet Joshua for the first time. We didn't know what to expect. We didn't even know if we would be successful in bringing him home. We didn't know how it was all going to work out, but we had faith that God was with us and that Joshua needed love.

As we boarded the plane, I thought about what we had committed to, and the doubts began to settle in with the reality. Fear tried to creep in as well. Martha and I prayed and talked about the many things that could happen and how we would respond to each one. But even with a plan there are still so many unknowns. The plane landed, and we were so excited we went straight to my aunt's home where Joshua had been staying for the last weeks. I walked into the room and he was in his crib, not making any noise. My heart sank as I picked him up for the first time. He was so weak, you could tell he had been through a lot. It's hard to put into words all the emotions swirling in my heart, but I knew clearly that Joshua would be our son. My wife and I cried both tears of joy and pain for Joshua. Seeing my beautiful wife holding Joshua for the first time was the first time I saw him smile.

The next hours went by quickly. We sat down with the caseworker and she explained all of our options. We could go through the system to adopt, which would take six months to a year, or we could hire a private attorney and expedite the process. We would have to forgo all the benefits that come with adoption like free college, etc., and have to pay out of pocket, but we could get him faster. We decided to go that route. We had a good friend recommend an attorney from Texas. We got on a plane without Joshua and the waiting began—so hard, but we knew that God was going to work it all out. In one month, God did a miracle and we brought Joshua home and adopted him. Our first son. WOW!

God took the broken thing in our life, the thing we thought was so messed up, the thing we thought might never be fixed and made a beautiful story.

We lost a baby and now we were bringing a beautiful angel home a year later.

Miracles continued to happen. Shortly after adopting Joshua Daniel Lopez, we had our second son, Cristian David Lopez. Cristian was in NICU for two weeks as a newborn and our faith was once again tested. This time, we knew and had confidence that God would see us through, just like He had in the past. God healed little Cristian and we had two healthy boys. Then, about three years ago, we had our little angel princess, Sofia Grace Lopez. Again, all I can say is WOW, just WOW!

Remember, the doctor had told my wife that we would never have kids, and we almost accepted that—almost, but God had a different story He was writing. Can you imagine the joy I felt, still feel to this day, when I look at my miracles? The impossibilities, the discouragements, all serve to help birth God's miracles in our lives. I love my family so much. They are my biggest blessings and accomplishments in life.

I have learned that no matter how many successes I have in business and ministry, no matter how many accolades I receive from people for my work, my music, or anything else I do, nothing will ever compare to the accomplishment of being a father and a husband.

I am a blessed man. I have had success in business, success as a songwriter and music artist, and fulfillment as a father and husband. I am living my dreams and it is only by God's grace.

CHAPTER 8

Forgiveness is a powerful thing when it comes to fulfilling our dreams.

WAVES OF FORGIVENESS

Forgiveness is a powerful thing when it comes to fulfilling our dreams. I knew that one day I would have to face one of the greatest giants that had ruled my heart for years: the un-forgiveness and hurt I had toward my dad.

> If you have ever had someone hurt you, if you have ever had someone betray you, if you have ever had someone wound you deeply, then you know that forgiving is not an easy task. It can be easy to say that you forgive, but to truly forgive in your heart is to experience freedom.

A few years ago, I received a call out of the blue from a friend of the family who explained in a brief phone conversation that my dad tried to commit suicide and that he was in bad condition at a VA hospital in Virginia. A great friend at the time, Tony Villani, told me: "I want to pay for your flight to go see your dad. I also want to give you some extra money so you can bless your dad the way you wanted him to bless you growing up." As grateful as I was for Tony's generosity, I have to admit that I was not excited about any of it, but I knew it had to be done. For God to place this on someone's heart, and for me to have an opportunity to see my dad was an answer to prayer. I just didn't feel ready.

All that said, I got on a plane and made my way to Virginia Beach where my dad was. It was awkward, at first. We didn't know what to talk about. I had not said I was sorry; he had not said he was sorry, so trying to make small talk just felt fake. After he was released from the hospital, I took my friend's advice and decided to take him shopping for some sunglasses. He had never owned a pair of good sunglasses. So, we were at the mall and I said to him, "Dad, I want to buy you a pair of Ray-Ban sunglasses."

He lit up with a smile and said, "Son, you don't have to do that!"

I said, "I want to, Dad," even though I struggled with it.

He picked out these very cool sunglasses and as we walked out of the store, he broke down crying. He turned to me and said, "Son, I am so sorry for not being a good father, I am so sorry for throwing you out of the house, I am so sorry for not showing you love, I am so proud of the man that you have become."

I had to take a breath. I didn't know what to say. He said words that I had been longing to hear for years. I told him, "Dad, I am sorry I was a rebellious son, I am sorry I didn't forgive you when you were trying to get help." We hugged it out and it was an amazing moment for us.

That day marked the beginning of a beautiful journey of healing for my dad and me. I wanted him to move back to Austin to be with his kids, but he had made his life in Virginia. We talked a few times a year and I can truly say that God completely healed my heart of all the anger and resentment I felt towards him. I learned what true freedom was. I didn't realize how much healing I needed from my relationship with my dad until I started living free of the pain. Forgiveness is such a powerful force. It can set your life on a completely different course. It can cause you to live without fear of rejection. It can cause you to enjoy life in a brand new way.

Dad and I had begun this beautiful journey of forgiveness and love. Although we didn't see each other often, we had a recurring conversation which went something like this: "Dad, move down to Texas, your kids love you and your grandkids want to spend time with their grandpa!" And he would say, "Next year." That went on for years until one day, he called and said he was ready to move down. I noticed in his voice that things were not okay. He had just gone through a bout with cancer and sounded very weak. When I picked him up, he was weak and looked like many years of pain had caught up with him. I immediately took him to the hospital to make sure he was okay.

It was December of 2015. After three hospitals, we finally got a diagnosis for his condition: pulmonary fibrosis, a disease that causes scar tissue around the lungs, making it hard to breathe. His doctor told us that he had two years to live. We hurried and got an apartment for him and started planning what the next two years would look like. Then another specialist gave us the correct diagnosis: he had only two months, at best. My five sisters, brother and

I were devastated. We were finally getting the opportunity to have the time we wanted with our dad and now he was dying.

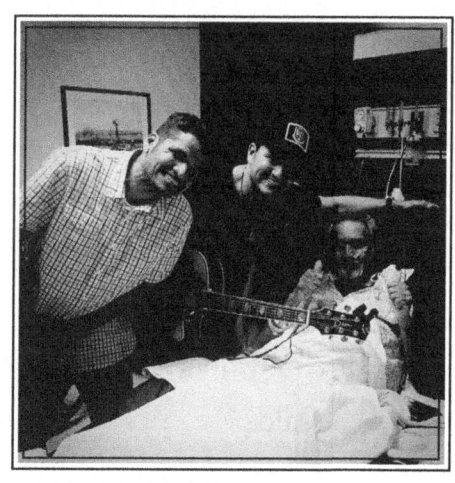

I spent every day with him at the hospital until he was ready to come home. My sister, Debbie, opened up her home for hospice. We gathered there for days. One night we decided to invite the entire family there with some of his friends. It was beautiful and straight out of a movie. We sang hymns and laughed. I remember thinking that night, here was my dad, who had lived a full life and all he wanted, in the end, was his family and friends surrounding him, laughing and singing. It was his dream come true. God once again showed His love and mercy. That night we knew that it was only a matter of time.

I sat by his bedside holding his hand. He could barely speak, but what he gave me were timeless gifts of wise words that will echo into generations to come. "Son, live fearlessly, be courageous, always forgive and above all, love with all your heart. Don't give up, son, don't you ever give up." Those words spoken by my dad, Josue Lopez Claudio, became the foundation for the rest of my life.

The following day, the hospice nurse spoke with my oldest sister and me. She said, "He is still holding on to something and doesn't want to let go. Does something need to be said?"

I knew exactly what needed to happen. You see, my mom had never told him that she forgave him, even though she had told us. My dad put my mom through a lot, and after they divorced my dad had carried the pain of this with him for years. She was the best thing that ever happened to him; it was something he could never seem to forgive himself for. My mom is the strongest person I know and her faith in God is so strong. She went over to my dad's bedside and whispered, "Cholo, I forgive you." This is what she called him when they were married. It was such a beautiful moment. Not more than a few minutes after those words, as I was holding my dad's hand, he went to be with Jesus.

That was March of 2016 and there is not a day that goes by that I don't miss him. He inspired me to write this book and to help others discover their potential. After my dad passed, everything that belonged to him became precious to me. Little things like his car keys, any of his writings, his songs, his instruments. Everything had a story. This made me think of leaving something for my kids one day. So, if this book only makes it into my kids' hands, I am happy with that. I want to give them something for the future. I want to inspire them to dream big, no matter what they face in life. I want to encourage them that God has a plan for their life just like He had one for my life. My dad inspired me to live the rest of my years with no dream un-pursued. To make the most of every moment and, when I fell along the way, to always get back up and keep fighting.

A year after my dad passed, I got invited to sing at a Campus Crusade National Conference at Moby Arena in Fort Collins, Colorado. After one of the nights, a man came up to me and asked, "Are you Josue Lopez's son?"

I replied, "Yes, yes I am."

He said, "I knew your dad. He helped me when I was addicted to drugs; he helped a lot of soldiers." He showed me a picture of over 30 soldiers that my dad had been helping in Virginia. I was in tears. Little did I know the impact that my dad had made on other people's lives before he passed. I took that unexpected meeting as a sign from heaven that Dad was okay. That his legacy would live on. Even though the enemy crushed him so many times, in the end, God's grace won. My dad died the wealthiest man at heart, surrounded by his family. No matter how many things we chase in life, the only thing that matters at the end is that we love Jesus and people.

> Today, start taking steps toward forgiveness. Start taking steps to freedom. Don't be robbed of so many beautiful moments that happen after forgiveness.

Whether you need to forgive yourself, receive forgiveness or forgive someone else, just forgive. It will set you free and set others free.

CHAPTER 9

You didn't come this far to quit, come on, give it your all!

FACING THE EYE OF THE STORM

When we think of BIG dreams, we think of finding love, the perfect spouse, having a family, a successful career, and making a significant impact on this earth with all the days that are given to us. For some, those dreams are for healing, recovering, getting past hurt and pain. Most of us also have other kinds of dreams, such as getting past our fears or feeding our need for adventure. Jumping out of a plane for the first time, climbing a high mountain, finishing a marathon—something that challenges us and takes us way out of our comfort zone. Some of us choose to face those dreams, while others steer clear of them. A few years ago, I had a dream that proved to be one of the toughest things I would ever do.

I have never considered myself an elite athlete, but I grew to love fitness in college and my greatest motivator now is my kiddos. I want to be able to live my best life for them, and that means staying healthy. And I still want to be able to run with them when I'm old! Years ago, I was given great advice from my friend, Don Losole, who is a coach. He said, as it pertains to fitness, find something you love and do it for the rest of your life. So, I did. I discovered that I loved all things outdoors: bicycling, running and swimming, and I began to train for triathlons.

My first triathlon consisted of a 400-meter swim, a 13-mile bike ride, and a 5k run. It was shorter than most triathlons, but I was dying. I was not prepared and I paid for it. Even a little kid passed me up—my ego was crushed. I said to myself, *I am going to train like never before and be in the best shape of my life.* I surrounded myself with people who were much better than I was, who helped challenge me to always be better.

A couple of months after that event, a friend suggested that I do the Ironman Triathlon: a 2.4-mile swim, 112-mile bike ride and a full marathon run of 26.2 miles, all in one day. Ugh—painful now to even think about it! Nervously, I signed up. By this time, I had finished a couple of Olympic distances triathlons, but this felt so far out of my reach that the only way I would be able to do it was with God's strength and lots of hard work. So, I went straight to work. I trained every day and sometimes two times a day. I prepared physically, mentally and spiritually for the next year. Physically, I had a plan where I would build endurance and what triathletes call, base. To do this I signed up for smaller races and specifically chose races that would challenge my stamina and endurance. My weekly workouts were 6 days of strategic cardio and interval exercise to help build my endurance and strength. My nutrition took a lot of planning. I had to consume the right amount of lean protein, complex carbs and healthy fats per day. I also had to stay very hydrated. I began to love this lifestyle especially because I felt so energetic. I was learning so much about my body, both physically and mentally.

The repetition of doing something productive where I would see great results motivated me to continue working hard toward my goal.

I would constantly listen to motivational podcast to motivate me. I also trained in places that would emulate the race course that I was going to race on. I knew that it would be very high elevation on the bike, open water swim and the run course would be very hilly. I found places to train where I lived that had this similar terrain. Finally, I surround myself with likeminded people. It is so important to surround yourself with people that challenge and motivate you to be the best version of you. My wife was so gracious and became my biggest fan, but some of my friends thought I was crazy for even signing up. One friend said, "Even if you don't finish, you're still a winner." This fueled me even more, because I knew that all the naysayers thought I couldn't finish.

The race was held in Coeur d'Alene, Idaho at one of the toughest courses I'd ever seen, with over 3000 feet of climbing on the biking and running segments. I decided to fly out early and train there for a few days so I could adjust to the altitude.

My coach told me four days before the race, "On the day of the race, there will be things out of your control, but you will always be able to control your response to those things."

Sure enough, two days before the race, a storm came through. And on the day of the race, there were 25-30 mile per hour winds. I prayed for good weather on race day, but it was the exact opposite. I think God knew that each obstacle was going to make me stronger. Sure, God could have calmed the storm, but He knew that I was going to learn something very valuable that would apply to all of life.

When I started the swim, athletes were being pulled out of the water because it was so choppy. I was terrified, but remembered the verse I had used throughout my training: 2 Timothy 1:7: *For God has not given us a spirit of fear, but of power and love and of a sound mind* (NKJV). It was true, the fear lasted for a few minutes and then courage filled my heart. I was focused and determined to finish the race. It was the hardest swim I've ever had to do—the water was so turbulent and very difficult, but somehow, I made it out of the water. I was off-balance but thrilled just to have finished the swim portion. For me, that was the scariest of the three! But I had no idea I was about to climb 3000 plus feet against 30 miles-per-hour winds on a light carbon bike.

The next hours were filled with pain, and God began to show me many parallels in my life with that race. I felt like giving up several times. One athlete who was right beside me as we were climbing said, "We're not going to make it," which only made me even more determined to finish.

I turned to him and said, "You didn't come this far to quit, come on, give it your all!"

Once again, his doubt fueled me to press harder, and I finished 113 miles on the bike. I was exhausted but knew the race was not done. As I got off my bike to run my first marathon, I thought, *You are one crazy Puerto Rican papa*! Yes, I laugh at myself a lot. It was just me and God on that run, and He began to show me so much about myself. I have been insecure all my life, always doubting myself. And I have always believed that I could not finish anything, but here was yet another thing that God was helping me accomplish. It was doing something for my confidence— awakening something I didn't know I had inside of me: perseverance, strength, and determination. I felt so alive on that run. Even though I was in complete pain and couldn't feel my legs, I felt freedom!

As I started the last mile there were tears in my eyes. I knew this was more than just a race for me. It was an opportunity for me to lean into what God had always believed about me, which is, *I can do all things through Christ who strengthens me.* As I crossed the finish line and heard the words, "Josh Lopez, you are an ironman!" I couldn't help but both tear up and smile big from ear-to-ear. My wife and I hugged and cried tears of joy together. It is hard to even put into words what I felt like. I was so happy I finished strong!

Finishing that race taught me lessons that have stayed with me to this day.

I can do all things through Christ who gives me strength!

Our body can do so much more than we tell it. If we believe, we can break barriers. Life happens so fast; we can spend a lifetime dreaming, or we can spend a lifetime living out these dreams. It's our choice to give up on them or give our all to see them come to pass. I believe with all my heart that God wants us to *live* our dreams and not just dream them. He knows our dreams can bring hope, healing, and love to others. When we accomplish our dreams we inspire others to attain their dreams and the gift continues to inspire others.

This life is hard and at times we have to face impossible things. We feel like giving up but we have a crowd of witnesses cheering for us in heaven. God is constantly showing up and reminding us that we are going to finish. We can do it with His strength. We can be everything He created us to be, even with our falls and breaks. We can live our best life because He believes the best in us. One of my favorite stories in the bible is found in Matthew 14. I want to make sure you get the complete story so here is the passage.

Matthew 14:22-32 NIV-"Immediately Jesus made the disciples get into the boat and go on ahead of him to the other side, while he dismissed the crowd. After he had dismissed them, he went up on a mountainside by himself to pray. Later that night, he was there alone, and the boat was already a considerable distance from land, buffeted by the waves because the wind was against it. Shortly before dawn Jesus went out to them, walking on the lake. When the disciples saw him walking on the lake, they were terrified. "It's a ghost," they said, and cried out in fear. But Jesus immediately said to them: "Take courage! It is I. Don't be afraid." "Lord, if it's you," Peter replied, "tell me to come to you on the water." "Come," he said. Then Peter got down out of the boat, walked on the water and came toward Jesus. But when he saw the wind, he was afraid and, beginning to sink, cried out, "Lord, save me!" Immediately Jesus reached out his hand and caught him. "You of little faith," he said, "why did you doubt?" And when they climbed into the boat, the wind died down.

I want to make sure you get the complete story so here is the passage. What a powerful story! We all go through storms and often times these storms take us to the deep and unknown. Jesus showed up at the least expected time and he also showed up in a way that scared the disciples at first. Sometimes in the middle of our chaos, Jesus will show up in ways that we never thought. It might be at a time when we least expect it. What is your storm right now? Is it a failed career, an illness, a failed marriage, a past mistake, a chronic pain, a lost loved one? The first thing Jesus told the disciples was to take courage! Whatever your storm is... take courage! Lift up your eyes and put them on Jesus. Believe that he has got you. The next part of the story is my favorite part. Peter began walking on the water toward Jesus. As long as his eyes were on Jesus he was doing the impossible, once he took his eyes off Jesus, he began to sink. It's true in our lives. We have to constantly keep our focus on Jesus. No matter what is happening around us, Jesus will cause us to walk above the waves and things that drown us. He is our help in time of need. He also knows that sometimes we will not do this. I'm so glad that even when we fall, even when we take our eyes of Jesus, even when we look at the bottom to hold us instead of Jesus...God will still reach out His steady hand and save us from drowning! God is faithful. He will never let us sink as long as we look to him. I encourage you to take your eyes off your present situation, take your eyes off the very thing that is causing you to sink and put your eyes on Jesus. How do we do this in a practical way? One of the things that I do when I am going through something tough is to make sure I am feeding my faith and starving my fear. I don't always do this initially but God is faithful to help me get to this point. In the world we live in now, it is easy to scroll on social media and watch the news and quickly fill our minds with fear. Instead, read your bible, read the promises of God, listen to a positive message. One of the other tools I use to help me focus on Jesus is worship. I love to sit at my piano at home and just sing songs to Jesus. My kiddos join in and we have church at home. You don't have to be a singer, you don't have to be a musician. Turn on some worship music and just say yes to God's presence. He is always ready. Worship him in your car, while you are running, in the kitchen while you are cooking, in your living room. Worshipping Jesus changes the atmosphere every time. You don't have to wait for Sunday church. In fact, I believe that you can experience God's presence in your life everyday. If you have never felt this indescribable peace, unchanging love and uplifting joy. I want to encourage you right now to invite Jesus into your heart. He can take all of your sin and give you a new heart.

John 3:16 says,

"God so loved the world that He gave His one and only Son, that whosoever believes in Him shall not perish but have everlasting life."

It's true! God loves you and there is nothing that you can do to change his love for you! He knows every detail of the storm that you are going through and He is reaching out his hand right now. All you have to do is reach back and take it. Pray this prayer right now if you want to receive Jesus into your heart;

Jesus, I am a sinner, and I ask you to forgive me. I believe you dies for my sins and rose from the dead. Come into my heart and make me new. Teach me how to love, how to follow you, how to trust you with all my heart. Amen.

If you prayed that prayer, I want to hear from you. I also encourage you to join a church and get around friends that will encourage you on this new journey. Keep your eyes on Jesus. You will get through life's storms, you will make it on the other side. God has you and will never let you go!

CHAPTER 10

There are times when God leaves a mountain right in front of us so we can grow stronger as we climb.

STREAMS OF GRACE

Have you ever asked yourself, what if I had not gone through the tough times that I went through? What if my life had been less dramatic, without so much hardship? I can tell you this, I am thankful for all of the hardships in my life. Each one represents a mountain that I have had to climb and, in the process, God has shown me some amazing things. He continues to do this today!

One of those hardships was the recession that hit in the early 2000s. I was still building my window covering business and my wife was a partner for a financial firm. I also led worship for a church, but even with several income streams, we were hit hard. Over the course of a year, as we tried to do everything we could to make ends meet, it seemed as though we were going deeper into financial crisis. I feared we might lose everything, and I would pray, *God make a miracle happen. Take this mountain of debt away.* I found out very quickly that life doesn't work that way.

Several times in life, I have found myself asking God to move a mountain, to remove the obstacle standing in the way of where I wanted to take my family. He certainly has all the power, He can do it in seconds. But the truth is, there are times when He leaves those obstacles and that mountain right in front of us so we can grow stronger as we climb. Because the only way we're getting to the other side is by climbing. So I began to climb. One of the first things I learned while I was climbing was that family was the most important thing. We had been doing so well financially for so long that our priorities were out of place. Hard times will shift your focus back to what is really important. Quality time with my family became priority, and I was also able to make several mission trips helping orphanages. It was so life giving!

We began to build our business smarter, manage our resources better and continue to find purpose in everything we did. Giving back became a priority for my wife and me. I began to read books on how to build a thriving business. I was a sponge around successful business men and women and I would take everything I could learn. We began to focus on not trying to do everything but becoming good at one thing. This was a game changer! We had been offering window coverings for many different clients, but now we began to focus on just commercial and luxury residential properties. Over the course of two years, we became the Restoration Hardware of window treatments. We cut out the things that robbed us of our family time and began to focus on a way that we could truly prioritize our family.

The two things that changed in the year after the recession were focus and finding our specific purpose. On every single job we put our best efforts forward. We built an incredible team and served amazing clients. God has blessed us in so many incredible ways, and each year we've grown by more than 25%. Now, we are able to give back to the community and make a significant impact. I was invited as a business owner, to the governor's mansion to sit down and talk with our governor about how we could make a difference in our community—an experience I will never forget!

It wasn't easy to get to where we are today and we are thankful every day for the success that God has given us. Looking back to that day when I was asking God to somehow give me a miracle and make it all go away, little did I know the answer was going to come in the form of hard work, focus, working smarter, providing excellent customer service, and consistency. God had been shaping those values in me for years, and because of the hard times we went through, they were finally able to grow.

I also began to see huge blessings with my music: the painful years were turned into lyrics with a melody. Huge doors began to open to share this hope with the world! I had the opportunity to do several big tours, sharing hope and life to people all over the US and abroad. I was able to release several music projects working with incredible friends. I got to be a part of a Dove Award-winning Spanish language album produced by my friend, Phil Sillas, and another that was nominated for a Grammy Award. I even wrote my first song for a movie!

Greatness began to be redefined for me. It was no longer about the accolades I received for singing on big stages, it was about doing something with purpose and making a difference in people. This was my fuel. So much of my music came from my broken places and now it was being used to help mend broken people. This has been a common theme throughout my life.

> To this day, I am amazed at how God takes the things in our life that were meant to break us and turns them into things that help mend others.

The truth is, we were never promised a perfectly put-together life. We were never promised a pain-free life. God knew that we have to go through pain in this life so he gives us His strength, and He provides streams of grace for the seasons when we experience pain. He gives us His Holy Spirit and wisdom to help us navigate the most difficult mountains that we have to climb. He gives us his love so we know that every step of the way we are loved, and that He will always catch us if we fail.

I am thankful for the hard times in my life because they have taught me strength. I am thankful for the disappointments because they have taught me consistency and getting back up. I am thankful for hurt because it has taught me what kind of person I want to be to others. It has taught me that only God can heal my heart. I am thankful for the rock bottoms, the valleys, the tough mountains...all of it continues to teach me that God will always come through.

No matter how difficult the mountain, God will help us climb. God will be our rope when we are sliding. He will be our firm rock when we feel we are losing ground. He will be our vision when we have lost our way. He is with us every step of the way. He will never leave us alone. We must look to Him always, and especially when we are climbing.

Yes, God can move the mountain but usually He invites us to climb. There is something so beautiful on the other side of the journey. Oh, the things we will learn! Oh, the places that He will take us! Oh, the many things He will show us! Deep in these mountains we are sure to find His streams of grace.

CHAPTER 11

We need people in our life to help us be the best version of ourselves.

DEEP IN THE OCEAN

What is your greatest obstacle in accomplishing your dreams? We all have battles and demons that we fight every day. Some of us battle with addiction, some of us battle with insecurities. Some of us battle with shame, guilt and the pain of poor choices. I have battled with all of these. But my greatest obstacles in life have been depression and fear.

Let's face it, we all go to the doctor when we are sick physically—it's second nature and our first response to seek help for physical pain. However, when we have a broken heart, a mental battle, or an emotional wound, many of us feel like we need to deal with it alone. It's hard for us to be vulnerable, especially in a culture where everything is painted so perfectly on social media. It's hard for us to let someone in to help us. It's easier to live with the pain and act like everything is okay. We would rather post a perfect picture than show who we really are because we fear we'll be rejected. The truth is we are loved no matter what. God sees the mess and He still sees the best.

It took years for me to really understand this truth. Depression started at a very young age. It began with rejection, and the feeling of not being good enough. My relationship with my dad contributed greatly to this, and feeling unloved by him was a deep root of depression for years. There were days when I didn't want to live, days where I didn't want to get out of bed. But God helped me overcome this with His promises and the truth I found in the Bible. I began to learn who I really was, and the simple truth that God does not make junk. He created me with a purpose. God used three specific things to help me overcome depression and fear, and they are the tools that I use today.

The first thing was knowing what God said about me in the Bible.

Statements like, *We are God's masterpiece. We are chosen. We are the head and not the tail. We are more than conquerors through Him who loved us. We are called. We are not forsaken. We are loved and nothing can ever change that. We were created and designed with a specific purpose.*

We have something to give this world. I began to really believe these things about myself and others, and to walk them out in faith. It wasn't haughtiness, but rather a posture of gratitude for what I was discovering about God's love for me. His love now meant everything.

The number one depression and fear-breaker for me was the fact that now Jesus lived in me. I no longer had to face things in my own strength, I had full access to do all things through Christ!

I am a world changer not because of anything good that I have done but because Christ lives in me.

This was one of my biggest aha moments. I began to sing with this confidence, to walk with this confidence. I am still learning how to *fully* walk in this confidence. But I am no longer that scared, insecure boy that walked with his head down.

The second, and one of the most powerful, practices that helped me overcome depression was surrounding myself with positive friends and family. Friends and family who told me what I needed to hear but also encouraged me to be better. I am so grateful for these significant people in my life. We were created for relationship, and we all need friends and family to help us fulfill our destiny. If you ever want to go about chasing a dream alone, that is exactly where you will end up—alone. These friends and family continue to challenge me and help me be all that God has created me to be.

Accountability is everything. We all have blind spots that only a true friend or family member can help us see. I have felt low and defeated at points in my life and God has used my friends and family to help me get back on track.

We need people in our life to help us be the best version of ourselves.

How do we know if someone is good for us? Ask your-self these questions: *Does this person bring out the best in me? Does this person encourage and inspire me to be all that God has created me to be? Does this person challenge me to do what is right?* If the answer is yes to all of these, then this person is someone I want in my circle. If the answer is no, then I can still love this person but not let their negativity detour me from my destiny.

When I first met my wife, she encouraged me to love God and others. She was the best example of what is was like to have a cheerleader cheering for the dreams that God had placed in my heart. When I make mistakes, she still somehow sees the best. She is so consistent. This is the kind of relationship we all need in our lives. When we find our-selves alone in the dark pit of depression, we need to find the people who will help us get out of this pit and walk out our calling. You can't do this one alone. You need people.

The third practice that helped me defeat depression was genuinely caring for others. At certain points in my life I have felt sorry for myself, and God has been faithful to show me that there was always someone in a more diffi-cult situation. Counting your blessings every day, the ones that we take for granted sometimes, is the best way to live.

Finding fulfillment in helping others and being the biggest cheerleader for other people's dreams is the pinnacle of life! It's such a great feeling when you have helped someone accomplish their dreams and expected nothing in return.

There have been many people who have done this for me and now inspire me to do it for others. A pastor once paid for my piano lessons because he believed in me. Thank you, Pastor Rob Koke. Another pastor gave me my first job as a worship leader and took a chance on me. Thank you, Pastor Randy Philips. Two very kind producers helped me finish my first album. Thank you, Tony Villani and Mark Townsend. A friend bought us groceries and gave us free tacos when we were hungry as kids. Thank you, John Alonzo. The first producer who believed in a song I had written, thank you Phil Sillas! Young adult pastors helped me navigate through my dad issues and be ready for the woman that God had for me. Thank you, Earl and Oneka Mcclellan. Thank you, Ray Jones, for helping me make a lifetime dream come true by recording two live worship albums. Thank you, Martha for always believing in me and always being a champion toward our dreams together.

My mom is such a great example of being a true servant and encouraging others to accomplish their purpose in life. My beautiful mom made so many sacrifices so that I would have something. She loves being in the background and championing others. She loves helping others fulfill their dreams and encouraging people. My dad also worked so hard and even though he battled with so much, he gave me things in life that I am so grateful for. Thank you, Mom and Dad. There are so many people that God has placed in my life to help me fulfill my purpose and destiny. To this day He continues to do this and I am beyond thankful.

I believe we were meant to thrive and help others thrive. Now, I want to do for people what people did for me. The reason I believe not giving up is so important is because people are inspired to keep on going when you stay the course. When we choose to run our race and live without fear, it helps others do the same. Even the people who rejected me, and people I felt betrayed by, helped me get to my destiny. God has an amazing way of working all things together for those that love Him and are called by Him.

CHAPTER 12

Don't you ever give up, not today, not tomorrow, not ever!

SUNSET, DREAM AGAIN

I am beyond grateful for so many dreams realized! I believe with all my heart that the best is yet to come! As I reflect back on that period of time when I wanted to end my life, or when I did not know what I was going to eat, or where I was going to sleep, when I had lost things that were close to me and when life didn't make sense and

I just wanted to give up, God did not give up on me. He did not let me give up.

Thank you, Jesus! He has always been the coach in the corner saying, "You have this, son!" He is the Father that

139

is present all the time, constantly lavishing love on us. He is the strong protector that keeps us from destruction when we follow Him. Even when we fight against Him, He is fighting for us. He is everything and He is the one who inspires me every day to never give up.

> You see, Jesus faced much greater adversities and suffering when He walked this earth but He chose to never give up.

He chose to give His all for you and me. He chose to give His life so we could live ours to the fullest! What an incredible opportunity we have, every single day, to live our dreams and be the best versions of ourselves.

My life has never been perfect, nor will it ever be, but it has always been held together perfectly by my perfect creator. He has been there no matter where I have been in life. He has lifted me out of the darkest places. He has restored my life over and over. He has provided beyond all my needs. He has made so many dreams come to pass. The highest pinnacle of love that I have ever experienced has been the love He has shown me. Love is all. Because we have received this unconditional, unchanging and unending love, we want to share it with as many people as possible. That is the culmination of anything we will ever accomplish here on this earth. Love is the greatest legacy we can leave.

Perhaps you find yourself in some of those dark places I mentioned in this book. Perhaps they look a little different but still symbolize the same pain. It may seem like you are gasping for air, but you will breathe normally again. It may seem like the whole world has forgotten about you, but you are loved and God wants you to know that. Don't ever doubt it.

> Don't ever doubt that you have a purpose and that God made you with that purpose in mind. You are unique and placed on this earth to do something significant.

> Let go of the past. Let go of shame. Let go of hurt. Let go of failure. Let go of unhealthy habits. Embrace the truth that is found in these simple words: **You are loved!**

Pain is inevitable, but how we respond determines what we will turn that pain into. We are building strength and grit so that when we overcome we can help others on their journey. When we work hard and do our part to achieve our dreams, we get to see God's promises fulfilled in our life. It may not be overnight. It might be years! It might be today or tomorrow. Whatever the time frame, the most important thing that we can gain from fulfilling the dreams that God has placed in our hearts is a deepened love for Jesus and a desire to lead others to Christ. Dust off your dreams, pick them up again. Dream again!

Set your mind on things that are eternal. We live in a culture that wants instant gratification. We picture dreams happening *to* us and not something that we make happen. It takes grit, hard work, unmovable faith, perseverance, passion, failure and the commitment to never give up on your dreams. How will you use the gifts that God has given you? How will you give your resources and talents back to God and others? How will you respond when it gets tough? How will you make sure that you stay on course and run your race with focus?

Whatever your situation, I want to encourage you with a few promises, lifelines that have helped me in some of my darkest days. The following verses from the Bible have helped me in times when I questioned my calling. In times when I felt like giving up. In times when I felt like I was alone. In moments when I didn't see myself the way God sees me. I hope they encourage you like they have encouraged me, over and over again.

When I have felt like I had no plan.

Jeremiah 29:11 (NLT)

For I know the plans I have for you, says the Lord. They are plans for good and not for disaster, to give you a future and a hope.

When I have felt the weight of crushing defeat or a broken heart.

Matthew 11:28-29 (NIV)

Come to me, all you who are weary and burdened, and I will give you rest. Take my yoke upon you and learn from me, for I am gentle and humble in heart, and you will find rest for your souls.

When I have felt like giving up or when I have felt weak.

Isaiah 40:29-31 (NLT)

He gives power to the weak and strength to the powerless. Even youths will become weak and tired, and young men will fall in exhaustion. But those who trust in the Lord will find new strength. They will soar high on wings like eagles. They will run and not grow weary. They will walk and not faint.

When I was barely making it, financially.

Philippians 4:19 (NLT)

And this same God who takes care of me will supply all your needs from his glorious riches, which have been given to us in Christ Jesus.

When I felt unloved and forgotten.

Romans 8:37-39 (NLT)

No, despite all these things, overwhelming victory is ours through Christ, who loved us. And I am convinced that nothing can ever separate us from God's love. Neither death nor life, neither angels nor demons, neither our fears for today nor our worries about tomorrow—not even the powers of hell can separate us from God's love. No power in the sky above or in the earth below—indeed, nothing in all creation will ever be able to separate us from the love of God that is revealed in Christ Jesus our Lord.

A note from the author

Our dreams were meant for a much bigger purpose than just pleasure and fulfillment. I think God placed dreams in our hearts so we could impact those around us. Our life experiences can bring healing where healing is needed, hope where there was once hopelessness, and joy where there was once sadness. The only way that we can bring that to others is if we have lived it and gained strength from that experience.

I challenge you to write down every dream you have, then start praying specifically for each one. Make a progress board where you see them every day, and write down things that you have contributed to reaching each one. There is so much value in seeing your dreams on paper every day. Make a plan and start working hard toward them. If you are already working hard towards them, stay the course. If you have given up, pick them up again and give them another shot. It's never too late.

Wake up the dormant dreams. Wake up the desires that were placed there by your creator. Your unique fingerprint and calling in life is meant to give hope to someone. You have a purpose. Rise above the pain and setbacks that have only come to push you away from your destiny. You have a mission. You were placed on this earth for a reason.

Dig, dig, dig until you discover it.

Push, push, push until you start seeing the light break through.

Pray, pray, pray to sustain it.

Work, work, work with passion and perseverance.

Give, give, give your all to see it come to pass and to inspire others.

Don't you ever give up, not today, not tomorrow, not ever!

Afterword

A Prayer:

Father, you are our dream maker from start to finish. You placed dreams in our heart and you help make them come true. You show us the way and give us the strength to work hard. I pray for the person that is broken and has lost hope. Help them climb the mountain in front of them. I also pray for the person who is working hard toward their dreams and continues to believe. Help them stay the course. I pray that you would help them accomplish these dreams in your time. Continue to give them practical tools each day to help them accomplish these dreams. Give them the strength to sustain them by the power of your spirit. Above all, I pray their dreams would be straight from your heart and that they would inspire many generations. That they would have purpose and that these dreams fulfilled would bring you glory and cause us to live and love you in the way that we were created for. I pray that giving up would never be an option.

May everything we do in this life be fueled by your compassion and love. May we love and know you more and bring you glory with our lives. Thank you for never giving up on us and help us to never give up.

Amen.

Acknowledgements

When I started on this journey to write my first book, I second guessed myself quite a bit. I stopped and started a bunch of times. I guess you can say this book is a good example of never giving up on a dream. After my dear father passed away I wanted to ensure that when I go on to be with Jesus, my kids have something that could inspire them to believe and never give up on their dreams. It started with that small seed my dad planted without knowing and turned into writing a book to inspire as many people as possible.

I would like to thank my wife, who is my biggest cheer leader and support. God knew what He was doing when he placed her in my life. I absolutely love you Martha and I am a better man because of you.

I would like to thank my beautiful strong kids, Joshua Daniel, Cristian David, Sofia Grace...you are my why and everyday you inspire me to want to live out my purpose. Thank you MOM, you are my rock and I love you with all my heart. Thank you for always showing me what it looks like to trust in Jesus. I would like to thank my sisters and brother for loving me even when I found it hard to love myself; Debbie, Lisette, Ruth, Tommy, Jennifer. I love you. I would like to thank my friends who gave me so much encouragement in the process of writing this book; Gabe Salazar, Stephanie Harrison, Henry Herrera, Cameron Arnett, Phil Sillas, Chris Sanchez. I would like to thank all my friends that helped me achieve incredible dreams throughout my journey; Jason Meekins, Aaron Kiefer, Tony Villani, Israel Houghton, Aaron Linsey, Terrance Palmer, David Cruz, Mark Townsend, Daniel Kinner, Ray Jones, Randy and Denise Philips, Rob and Laura Koke, Sam and Kelly Mata, David and Rebekah Contreras, Earl and Oneka Mcclellan, Bryan Smith, Michael W. Smith, Calvin Nowell, Phil Sillas, The Guerra Family, Jerry Caldwell, Danny Chambers, Joel Osteen, The Katinas, Danny Gokey. I am beyond grateful that God has granted me the dream to work with these amazingly gifted friends.

Thank you God. All of my dreams, aspirations, accomplishments, purpose in life come from you and are for you Jesus. You always give us the strength to never give up. To you and you alone be all the glory forever!

For more resources

VISIT DONTGIVEUP.ONLINE

FOR DON'T GIVE UP RESOURCES

STREAM DON'T GIVE UP MUSIC

ON ALL DIGITAL MUSIC PLATFORMS

FOLLOW US

ON SOCIAL MEDIA

@JOSHDLOPEZ

Made in the USA
Coppell, TX
14 August 2020